Cows, Cars and Rucksacks

Cows, Cars
and Rucksacks

Magnie Shearer

The Shetland Times Ltd.
Lerwick
2011

Cows, Cars and Rucksacks

ISBN 978 1 904746 70 6

First published by The Shetland Times Ltd., 2011.

Printed and published by
The Shetland Times Ltd.,
Gremista, Lerwick,
Shetland ZE1 0PX.

Contents

Dogs and Exercise 1

Giraffes and Glasses 4

Great Balls of Fire 7

Hands On Driving 11

Two Travel Tales 15

New Words 19

Musical Abilities 23

Here, Kitty, Kitty 27

Snow Crisis 32

It's Curtains for All of Us 36

Homeward Bound 41

Sport for All 47

Hotel Aerobics 52

Wii and Me 59

Roll Me Over 63

About the author

Magnie Shearer was born and brought up in Lerwick, Shetland, and for over 40 years worked within the Isles. He is married with a family, two grandsons, and an adopted cat named 'Elwood'. He now lives in Levenwick and his previous book was entitled Cats, Clouds and Flatpacks (2009).

Dogs and Exercise

I enjoy walking. Partly this is because it has two elements to it. One, as I say, it's enjoyable; and two, it keeps me alive. This is a pretty good reason for doing it. Walking is all part of my cardio rehab programme. Nothing medically empowered, just a concept that I have come up with that gives me the exercise I need to keep the old damaged ticker running along, and which at the same time is an enjoyable pastime.

During the summer, especially, it is very pleasant here at Levenwick walking along the beach and up and around the headlands, or occasional forays down to Sumburgh and a walk from the lighthouse back to Grutness, playing tag with all the cars! I also like a walk circumnavigating the four or five miles around the streets of Lerwick, iPod wired to my head, music or an audio book playing, and losing myself in this world as I stride out. Then again, just simply walking, savouring the scenery, letting my mind wander and enjoying the sociable moments as I meet up with folks en route.

One thing I have discovered is that you make friends with a lot of dogs en route. I have no problem with dogs and have always enjoyed their company, and now they seem to hang around and wait for me to arrive. Some even bring me presents, like the black Labrador who always gives me an empty crisp packet. I have no idea where he finds them, but religiously, every day I pass, he sees me coming and trots off around the back of the house and, proud as punch, meets me as I walk past, with front paws on the fence rails leaning forward to donate his gift of the day. If I'm right, and he does this to everyone who passes, these folks have got a great scheme going here. Who needs those green, purple and white recycling bags; just get your dog to hand out your rubbish to passers-by?

Games are an important part of a dog's life and the mongrel collie that arrives at the gate with his saliva-encrusted ball, beseeching me to throw it back down the path falls into this game-playing category. This, if you do it once, will tie you up for hours as this beast is as fast as lightning and, no sooner have you thrown it, than he's back again drooling over the gate, eyes imploring you to 'do it again'. If, like me, you're soft on animals, then rather than leave this sad, old fellow hanging out over the road, you end up creating a sort of trial-by-speed scenario whereby you try to catch him out by throwing the ball into some bushes, or some such thing, to give you the chance to dash away far enough so he can't see you on his return – or at least you feel that he can't see you – and you can continue your walk. However, sometimes this develops into a mind game of wits as you battle it out with a large hairy dog. Eventually you think you've won and, having thrown the ball as far as you can into his folk's garden, having crouched down behind the gate, on the pavement, beside the main road, you leap up in delight, punch the air, and run off along the pavement straight into the owner and his wife returning to their house. They, having seen the whole episode from a distance as they approached their home with caution, are slightly bemused by the sight of a grown elderly man leaping about outside their gate, apparently throwing things into their garden, shouting and hollering, while punching the air and then running away. It took a moment to explain and while they could confirm they had a dog, the whole ball-throwing incident seemed to faze them somewhat. I now walk on the other side, while the collie hangs out over the gate, salivating furiously as I tiptoe past.

Then there's the old spaniel that, on seeing me approach, throws back his head and howls out his version of Meatloaf's *Bat Out of Hell*. Nobody else gets this. I've watched him, he just gives them an uninterested muffled bark, but on seeing me I get the full works, chorus and all. He does the hair bit as well, as he rocks back and fore with his great big floppy ears swinging to the head-banging routine. It's worth seeing, if a tad embarrassing, as folk stand and stare at this rocking spaniel and me. I'm sure they think I've maltreated him in some way, until I point out his tail wagging furiously in time to his howls.

Finally, of course, there's the one which shoots out the front door, blunders through the bushes, crashes up against the wall hanging his head and arms over the top, tongue hanging out and I give his ears a pull, squeeze his nose and give his hair a quick ruffle and a slap around the head. He seems to enjoy this; and so does his dog, which calmly arrives on the scene some moments afterwards and sits there, with his deep soulful eyes looking up at me, as if to say: *"God knows what I did to deserve him."*

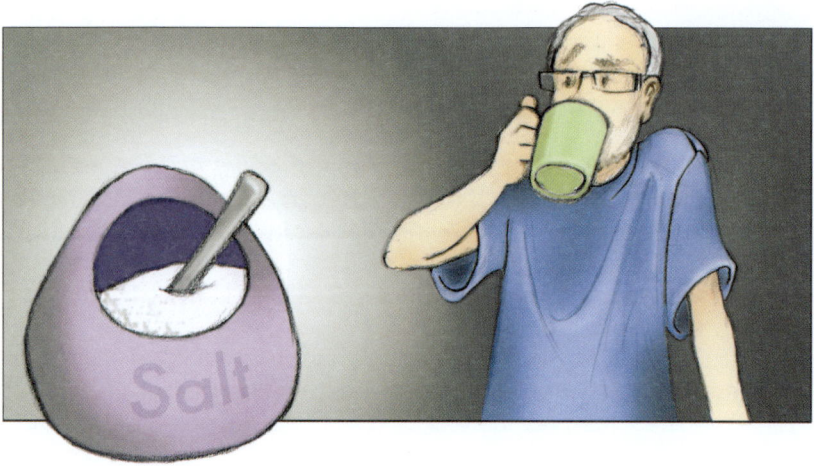

Giraffes & Glasses

I have just heard on the radio, that giraffes have no vocal chords. I empathise with the giraffe. Think Melman from *Madagascar* (forget the hypochondriac tendencies, just watch him moving). He's long of leg and seems to be quite a tall animal that appears to have a problem getting clothes to fit him. Our oldest grandson has a book entitled *Giraffes Can't Dance*, by Giles Andreae, which we both enjoy a lot as, although he dreads the annual Strictly Come Jungle Dance, in the end Gerald becomes a winner.

I thoroughly enjoy a birl too, but in some dance routines my style is not unlike Gerald the giraffe. On one occasion, during a Canadian Barn Dance (in the wee small hours of Up-Helly-A' morning, admittedly) my feet and clapping were totally out of sync and the whole thing sounded like Thomas the Tank Engine was coming down the hall... clappity clap... clappity clap... so much so that, as I recall, I was politely asked to leave the floor. Or, at least, the suggestion was made that we had danced enough and could maybe sit down for a wee while. I'm actually quite proud of that. Not many people are so out of sync with the music that it's better for all that they retire gracefully from the scene.

Singing is another of those mercurial moments in life; you either have a great talent for it or, like some of us, you are best left out of the room altogether. I seem to find that singing comes naturally, elegantly, and without any stress or strain around 3am in a 50-seater bus as you wind your merry way around the town on the last Wednesday morning in January. I have even been known to lead the lyrics and 'solo' on the chorus at times!

However – and I'm not being irreverent here – when you find yourself at, say, a wedding, or even a funeral, and a beautiful hymn is laid out before you, all knowledge of keeping a tune in any form of rhythmic formation flies right out the window. Occasionally, there is a strong singer to your right or left. You manfully try to keep up, only to be knocked sideways when, getting into the flow of things, getting louder by the minute and, in your mind, matching them note for note, they suddenly stop... and you, you alone, are left to belt out the last line of the verse, much to the horror of those standing next to you. Why do these folk who can sing so well do that?

You then revert to that 'man thing' whereby you stand erect and, looking forward with all confidence, mime the words. Or at least I'm sure some do, as having stood next to someone who, only minutes before was giving it laldy, suddenly I'm aware that the lips are moving but no sound emits, while I struggle on out of tune, out of key, but determined to finish the verse. Now, as I say, I've discovered that giraffes have no vocal chords. That maybe helps to explain a few things – long legs, tall, can't dance, can't sing... Hmm!

Life is full of little ups and downs like that and now, as those dark mornings creep up on us again as winter approaches, there are other little moments which are set to try us.

One of the more bizarre of these happened the other week, when I arrived at the office and switched on the computer only to discover that I was wearing the 'wrong' glasses. When I say 'wrong', that's not strictly correct, 'different' would be a better description. Somehow, in the semi-darkness of the morning, when both my mind and my eyesight are not at their optimum level, I had picked up the 'second' pair that was lying beside the bed. I guess you are on automatic mode at this weird hour of the morning and, while all around sleep soundly on, you blunder around the house in total darkness grovelling for light switches and such like.

Breakfast is a pantomime really, you pour out your daily dose of cereal, the stuff your dietitian swears is the best thing for controlling your cholesterol and so a wondrous thing. To my mind, a small shovelful of dry oat flakes lying in the bottom of a bowl at half-six on a dank winter's morning is hardly the 'pick-me-up' I need. I faff around buttering my side-plate and loading the dishwasher with slices of toast; my cup of tea has a distinctly different flavour and it takes me a moment to realise I have made a mug of steaming liquid and steered in a heavy quantity of sea salt from the open bowl which lies beside the hob. I even brushed my teeth in front of the mirror for goodness sake, and never noticed.

I'm now toying with the idea of sticking a post-it note on my forehead with a short but subtle check-list for those times in the early hours when I'm not at my best. Headings such as: 1 – Glasses; 2 – Trousers; 3 – Shoes, etc. This may give me a bit of a fright when I look in the rear-view mirror while driving into work, but I'm sure it will be worth it. It seemed to be successful for the TV remote control, after I stuck a post-it on the fridge door with the words *"Look in here"* in large letters scrawled across it!

Great Balls of Fire

Firstly I should probably introduce myself. I am Elwood. Elwood J. Blues, harmonica and vocals. My brother, Jake E. Blues, was the other half of the team. We are two dude cats, separated soon after birth, and we have gone our separate ways in life. Of Jake, I have no idea what became of him. That's what happens to cats. We are an independent breed who live a life of relative freedom, compared to dogs that are carried, led, fed, bred and made to take part in other human-designed activities. We cats, on the other hand, occasionally slip in and out of humans' lives in a kind of semi-destructive way, and so make our presence known.

I was originally cared for by my current owners' daughter, who lavished enormous amounts of care and affection on me, and I kindly returned this love by inflicting a cat dust/hair aversion of huge proportions on her other love, namely her partner. This resulted in me being adopted by her father and his long-suffering wife. At least that is what they think. I actually adopted them, and they in turn have yet to agree the terms of our co-habitation, but they will eventually see the main conditions I've set are right and proper and come round to my way of thinking.

That, therefore, is the basis of my existence etc. I like to think my mother was an errant Siamese of good breeding, and my father a randy Tom who happened to be passing by. I have inherited my mother's good looks, and possibly a slight smattering of my father's 'streetwise' cunning and panache. I fear I may well have also picked up the genes from my grandfather's stupidity and, in some cases, a hell of a lot of them. This is not good. It has little or no kudos in the big wide world, and you will see that this has a large bearing on all that I do and all that happens to me.

Suffice to say, this little tale of Fire and Water is a case in point. I generally find weather a phenomenon I could do without. I don't need seasons. I need sun and warmth. Snow is not in my list of plusses. Ok, I do sometimes let myself slip and find rare moments of fun and excitement in snowy days, where I accompany the man of the house in his moments of madness, and we sledge down the hill together. He then carries me back up to the top of the hill on the back of the said sledge, which he finds highly amusing and, of course, I find very satisfying and saves me ploughing through the deep drifts. Good combo.

This particular day I had been out for a small ablution moment, and to say it was cold is not the word, it was bloody freezing and my whole head and body was a freeze zone. I blundered back into the house and took up residence directly in front of the Rayburn: an essential item in every cat home. However, Mrs Boss was busy cooking soup and I appeared to be in the way. How that could be I just cannot imagine, but I was summarily shoved through to the sitting room. I made a mental note to rub up along her black newly ironed jeans, just so we understood who was really the Boss around here.

I sauntered casually into the sitting room, giving her one of my 'looks' as I passed, and wandered through towards the mulberry coloured rug in front of the fire. A good spot of back rolling, leg waving, head rubbing ensued and I then sat up and, satisfied I'd left enough hairs to merit a comment and a Hoovering session tomorrow morning, I stretched out and dozed fitfully. After a moment, although

I felt comfortable, I was still suffering the effects of squatting down on my haunches in the wet, cold snow. I decided to take up position closer to the wood burning stove: a thing of beauty and delight. It was in full furnace mode, having just had a load of wooden logs supplied; it crackled and spat, and so I edged nearer and sat there staring at the glowing red embers and absorbing its warmth and cosiness.

I may have dropped off for a brief moment, but the next thing I knew I was grabbed from behind, hoisted in the air, and the room was filled with the cries of *"Oh my God... look at the cat!"* and *"For the love o' God, what a stupid animal!"* And one phrase which did attract my attention more than the rest... *"Quickly, fill the basin with water, his head's on fire!"*

I have to say I was slightly aware of a burning hair sensation and, more accurately, a slight singeing smell wafting through the air as I was transported, at some speed I might add, through to the kitchen. This manoeuvre seemed to fan the flames, so to speak, and I have to say I was quite annoyed at being grabbed in such a violent manner, and lashed out at my carrier. I managed to leave my mark on his bare arms, so we both understood my annoyance and, unfortunately, he seemed to tighten his grip even more.

"He's not going to like this, but it's all we can do!" Well, he got that bit right. We sailed through into the kitchen and, in a moment of sheer madness, he upended me and plunged me head first into the basin full of water. What the hell did he think he was playing at! For God's sake, cats and water... not a combination you want to play around with. There was a loud hissing sound as my head disappeared into the bowl, and a further loud hissing sound as I re-emerged. The first was from the burning hair and the second from my mouth. I lunged desperately at the idiot that was holding me and managed to inflict an open wound on his other arm and then set about systematically wiping every dish, cup, pot, pan, utensil, and cutlery from the kitchen drainer as I made my escape. He had by now slipped his grip on me and was dancing around the room, waving his arms about like a windmill, and she in turn was chasing after him shouting something about *"blood everywhere"* and to stand still.

I took a calculated risk and leapt from the drainer, soaking wet, and abseiled down the towels onto the floor, skittered across the wooden floor and made my escape towards the bedroom. Always a good safety position, as being old and becoming infirm they cannot always get down to crawl underneath the bed and get hold of me, unless truly desperate. I generally just lie there for a while until they are both down on all fours, crawling in, and then just leap towards their heads; they in turn shoot upwards and crack themselves on the bed planks and in the confusion that follows, I simply walk over the top of them and out of the room. It works every time. You would think they might learn, but no, not ever.

After an hour or so, I ventured out and casually lay in the sitting room doorway and listened to the conversation. I gathered, after a moment, they were discussing me...

"I saw him, he just was sitting there with his eyes closed, leaning slowly forward."

"What, was he asleep then?"

"Yes, fast asleep... then he just leaned a bit too far and fell slowly against the stove, with his forehead firmly clamped up against the side."

"Why didn't you shift him?"

"Well, I didn't think the stupid thing would just lie there. I thought he would spring back when he realised he was burning, but he just lay there, his eyes closed, his head burning and a little wisp of smoke slowly rising upwards from his forehead!"

'Stupid thing...' That's no way to refer to your pet... another mental note to sit on his newly washed car next weekend, after I've walked through a couple of puddles first.

So, so... seems I may have inadvertently fallen asleep headfirst into the side of the wood burning stove, and obviously caused a minor incident that escalated into something resembling a small nuclear war the way it was being portrayed by the humans. I did notice that the soup was no longer in the pans, there appeared to be a few broken plates in the waste bin, and virtually all the walls and floors in the kitchen had been scrubbed, though the tell-tale specks of red seemed to linger on every one.

Hmm... I slipped outside for a while and had a sleep in the garage until the dust settled, and then He was out in the morning whistling on me, with a bowl of fresh new biscuits.

Nice one, Elwood.

Hands on Driving

This is going back somewhat to the late sixties and the days before cars all had indicators fitted, though some did have a small arrow thing that protruded from the side of the vehicle and clunked up and down beside your head. There are enough problems today with some comedians driving and speaking on their mobile phones, or worse still texting, and the law demands you keep your hands on the wheel. However, thinking back a while, there was a time when you were actively encouraged to steer with one hand while doing bird impressions with the other. This actually formed part of your official driving test, and was fully condoned by the Highway Code.

Hand signals, as they were formally known, were an integral part of driving and had three main functions. One, where you wound down your driver's window – no electric systems then-a-days – and stuck your arm out and pretended you were a disabled, one-armed seagull coming into land, by flapping it up and down vigorously. This procedure informed those behind you that you were intending to slow down and stop. It could also mean you had a piece of gum stuck to your fingers, or you were just trying to empty the ashtray. Hence the confusion at times.

A similar bird-like manoeuvre consisted of once again sticking your arm out the window and, in a style not unlike a ballet dancer or a musical conductor, you deftly rotated your hand forwards in a circle. This, believe it or not, told the folks behind and in front of you that you were turning left.

Another clever trick you were allowed to do was just stick your arm straight out the window, with your thumb uppermost and the flat of your hand vertical, so that on narrow streets you could smack the folk on the opposite pavement across the back of the head. This was to tell them you were turning right.

There were another two or three which you were supposed to do inside the car. One, I recall, had you holding your arm directly across your face with your hand pointing left. This told a traffic policeman on point duty, or an approaching car, that you were going to move left. If you actually could see them! Driving one-handed with your arm across your face restricted your vision somewhat.

Driving was quite a hazardous business back then, and in the winter very cold, as you flapped your way around corners, waving frantically as the snow blew in through the open windows. Cocooned inside our air-conditioned vehicles with push button computerised flashing indicators everywhere has certainly taken the exhilaration and animation out of driving nowadays. Gone are those happy moments where you met up with others at junctions, all of you steering recklessly one-handed, waving manically out of windows like a flock of demented geese, honking at one another before shooting off down another road in a haze of blue smoke. Parp, parp, as Noddy would say...

Forty years or so ago driving was a whole lot different, and in some ways relatively more exciting. None of these clever aids to navigation fitted to your dashboard, with an inane sounding woman telling you to turn round because you've missed a turning... though, come to think of it, sometimes we had the real thing sitting in the back.

Then, there were the main controls of the car. Nowadays, the gear lever is attached to a fully synchronised set, maybe as many as six gears, whereas then you had three, possibly four, and only one of them synchronised. Instead, there was a lever as long as a flagpole which you gripped fiercely and waved about inside the car, eventually making contact with the cogs down below and, hopefully without too much grinding, engaged the two, which resulted in some forward motion.

The steering wheel was the size of a cart-wheel and took somewhere around five or six complete turns to manoeuvre the vehicle in a complete circle. You spent days unwinding and winding the blessed thing from side to side as you drove along the narrow twisting roads. No power steering then; if you drove a truck or a bus you had biceps to rival the best all-in wrestlers. The tyres were about as wide as a cigarette packet and the wipers, if vacuum powered, were a laugh. They struggled to make it across the windscreen and flapped about as if on their last dying breath.

One of the more lugubrious things about the loss of those cars was the passing of the front bench seat and the column change gear lever. These innovative mechanics assured you could seat three in the front and, by gripping firmly and beating furiously – a bit like mixing up an egg in a bowl – a lever which stuck out from the side of the steering wheel, at some time the thing would engage with a gear, via some rods and joints, and away you would go.

No seat belts; so on corners with only two in the front your passenger and you could get quite intimate, while on opposing corners the driver could find himself staring out through the middle of the windscreen, while hanging on grimly to the steering wheel. The seats in these old saloons were generally polished leather, which made those sliding movements all the more graceful.

The choke lever was an all-important part of starting a vehicle. This clever little device meant the petrol/air mix could be adjusted manually so that on starting the car on a cold day you pulled it right out and, on pushing the starter button, with a rumble and a bang, away she would go. After a few minutes, you pushed the choke in a bit to reduce the mixture and also to let the folks behind you see where they were going as, inevitably, the full use of the choke meant you had built up a wall of blue smoke which often engulfed the car and those behind for days!

Now we have cars that can self-steer themselves into parking spaces, tell you when you are too near to the one behind, are air-conditioned, have wall-to-wall sound systems, DVD players in the headrests, and control everything within the engine compartment via a mini computer chip. We had none of these, and most of the chips were from the Viking Café and came with a pineapple ring covered in batter; and the sound system was six of you in an old A35 van singing on your way to a regatta dance in Walls.

Two Travel Tales
Car Singing

I know you've all done it. I can imagine that some of us are a lot better at it than others. As far as I know you still cannot be arrested for doing it alone in a car. I, too, have crooned my way through the highways and byways, belting out my version of Ray Parker Jnr's *Ghostbusters* or an old powerhouse version of Queen, Meat Loaf, Lady Gaga or, dare I admit it, an Abba song.

Now, here I'm probably showing my age, but on Radio 2 in the afternoons, Steve Wright plugs various folks' 'non-stop oldies' for around a half an hour. Some choices are dire, but everybody's likes are different, so that's fair enough and even among the 80's horrors there are a few good old sing-a-long ones.

The problem I have is that this often coincides with my southbound travel through the village of Cunningsburgh. Nothing outwardly wrong in that, but the timing could be better.

When the schools are in session, this time of day is usually when the mums, dads, grans etc., are collecting their bairns from the school. Now, when this happens, the speed limit is reduced, and rightly so, to 20mph, but 20mph is not a good speed to trundle through when I am in full voice.

Take 'Amarillo' for example, a jolly little song to join in with, and I'm getting into the swing of it with gusto, then the lights start to flash, down I crawl to a sedate 20mph, but I'm still giving it my all. The mums are all walking along the pavement directly beside me, and meantime I am just getting to the "Sha-La-La" bit, rocking in my seat, joining in full voice. Then I notice out of the corner of my eye the startled look spreading across their faces. They begin to gather their offspring closer to them, and edge towards the fence and away from the road as this guy in a car seems to be shouting, head jerking, air punching, wheel drumming, by himself, all alone, nobody else with him, not even a dog. Such is the success of modern car comforts, no sound emits and to all intents and purposes the driver appears to be having a small seizure.

So, therefore, my car singing has had to be restricted, and now as I glide past on my way home, I smile politely and continue on my journey, only to resume my performance later en route. "Sha-la-la la-la la-la-la... Sha-la-la..."

Sleepy Trains

I enjoy train journeys, especially European train journeys, and hopefully some day I'll maybe traverse other continents by train. It's a civilised, relaxed mode of transport, where you sit and see the back gardens of a myriad of folks who'll you never meet, but wish you could. For no other reason than to ask them why they keep an 8ft blow up shark on their shed roof, or what would seem to be the main wing of a small commercial airliner below their gazebo.

I long to stop and meet these guys, as apart from the absurdity of having them, I just would love to hear their version of how they acquired these items and, even more exciting, how they managed to get them into the back gardens of their terraced houses.

"Excuse me... I've just moved in next door, and I have a small 8ft shark I need to get into my garden, could I possibly come through your living room?"

"Oh, hi... you don't mind if this crane lifts the 747 wing over the roof of your house into my garden, do you? ... Well, the wife was watching Diarmuid Gavin on the telly last week and she's designed this garden water feature using an aeroplane wing..."

The list is endless, and you never get that flying or even travelling by bus or car. There's also the added bonus that you can arrive at the station minutes before your train leaves, board the carriage and find your reserved seat and settle down in comfort. Nobody wants to search through your underwear, throw away your toothpaste because it's a terrorist threat, or fondle you in a manner which is just 'too friendly' for complete strangers on their first meeting. There's also none of this 'before you move off stuff' where a smile-school graduate spends a considerable time explaining what to do if you find yourself in a life and death situation. You're also allowed to get up, wander about, go and buy a beer or a sandwich, and spray the folks sitting opposite you with small particles of food or liquids. Enormous fun, trains.

The downside, I find, is the probability that I will fall asleep. It must be the motion of the train and possibly the simple monotony of travel itself, but fall asleep I assuredly do. This is not good. I am not what you would call a fetching sleeper. At night, in bed, different thing altogether, I fall asleep like a baby, curled up in the foetus position, and doze fitfully but quietly and comfortably till morning or nature calls me out of my slumber. Dozing on trains is a world apart. I tend to slip slowly down the seat, my legs spreading wide as my head slumps onto my chest, my mouth opens and I believe I may even start to drool slightly. I begin to breathe like a gorilla on heat, with huge sighs and snorts, then stop altogether and lie there without a movement apparently, no breathing, no chest heaving, nothing.

The folks opposite begin to lean forward towards me, certain

I have just departed this life, when I suddenly emit a shrill cry and shoot forward before collapsing back onto the seat again. This causes a near cataclysmic moment in the carriage, as they drop their polystyrene cups of soup or throw packets of crisps skywards. I awake to this mayhem, and in a sleep-induced stupor look around me to find folks sitting, standing, apologising to one another, wiping their clothes, faces, carriage windows, seats etc., etc., and I come to the conclusion that we have had a major shunt of sorts.

"What's happened?" I ask the old guy sitting next to me, whose forehead is a bright tomato red colour and his smart taupe-coloured M&S jacket seems to have an assorted selection of coleslaw festooned across it.

"What's happened!" he shrieks at me…*"What's happened! You've just ruined my jacket, that's what's happened!"*

"But… I was asleep…" I say.

New Words

The late, great Douglas Adams (*Hitch Hiker's Guide to the Galaxy*) once wrote that in life there are many hundreds of common experiences, feelings, situations and even objects which we know all about and recognise, but for which no words exist. On the other hand, the world is littered with thousands of spare words which spend their time doing nothing but loafing about on signposts pointing at places. His idea was that we should get these words down off the signposts and into everyday conversation.

With that in mind, and using his original concept, while driving around the Isles I thought that there are a few signposts and names of places here that we could introduce into our language and conversation.

Aywick: The single bristle that sticks out sideways on a cheap paintbrush.

Bannaminn: The panic caused by half hearing a Tannoy in an airport.

Blosta: Generic term for anything that comes out in a gush despite your best efforts to control it, e.g. – tomato ketchup, petrol, wind etc.

Burwick: The way a fat person's cheeks move when you drive over a cattle grid really fast.

Clickimin: Old Roman name for a ticket collector at the Colosseum.

Clumlie: A leg which has gone to sleep and has to be hauled around after you.

Da Beorgs: A rumbling condition sometimes encountered after eating foreign food on holiday.

Dore Holm: These are doors that open the opposite way to what you expect.

Drongs: To hold a ruler on the end of a table and make the other end go bbddbbddbbrrbrrrrddrr.

Elvis Bay: The original name for the online auction website before Col. Parker threatened to sue.

Eshaness: The residue left on the community hall floors after a Folk Festival bagpipe and whistle concert.

Fladdabister: The mark left on your sunburned thighs when rising from a plastic chair.

Fugla: One of those irritating, handle-less, slippery, transparent plastic bags you get in supermarkets to put your fruit in, which no matter how you hold them, always let something fall out.

Funzie: Descriptive of a drunk person's attempts to be endearing.

Gloup: The behaviour of your lips when trying to spit out mouthwash at the dentists.

Gossabrough: The push-taps in airport toilets that enables the user to wash their trousers without actually getting in the sink.

Gluss: The noise made by someone who has just been grossly flattered and is trying to make light of it.

Grindiscol: Educational establishment that Mavis went to.

Grinigeo: Young men who stand around smiling at weddings as if to suggest they know the bride rather well.

Gruney: The look someone gives you by which you are aware they're too drunk to have understood a word you've said during the last 20 minutes.

Grutness: The noise, like a pig, that escapes with uncontrollable laughter.

Hamarberg: To tap ones index finger against the glass of an aquarium in an attempt to communicate with a Tiger Fish.

Hascosay: The expression used by people feigning interest in the latest gossip while they are actually desperate to hear more.

Hols O' Scraada: The tiny depressions in a piece of Ryvita

Jarlshof: Old Norse word for a computer spelling mistake.

Laxobigging: The frightening result of eating one to many prunes.

Mangaster: A fitted elasticated bottom sheet which turns your mattress banana-shaped.

Mavis Grind: The almost completely forgotten girlfriend from your distant past.

Muckle Ossa: The never forgotten girlfriend from your distant past.

Moull: The collective name given to a small random but happy group of cows.

Moull of Eswick: A comic horror fantasy film with Jack Nicholson, starring Cher, Susan Sarandon and Michelle Pfieffer as the three cows.

Ocraquoy: The ancient Eastern art of being able to fold road maps properly .

Papil: What babies do to soup with their spoons.

Quarff: That kind of facial expression which is impossible to achieve except when having your passport photo taken.

Rompa: To walk or hike in a joyous manner over hill and dale with no sense of direction.

Scuddillswick: The mess of wires and cables behind your TV, DVD and satellite box in the corner of the sitting room.

Sligatu: Pretending not to be in when the Jehovah's Witnesses, Mormons or Halloween Guizers call along.

Snarravoe: Adjective which describes the behaviour of Sellotape when you are tired.

Stebbligrind: The word used to describe the moment you walk into a wall while negotiating a route from the bedroom to the bathroom in the dark.

Tingon: The noise made by a light bulb which has just shone it's last.

Trumba: The type of fart you know will be talked about for a while after.

Twageos: The two little lines that come down from your nose.

Vestinore: The name given to undergarments worn by men with nasal problems.

Uyea: The tiniest inkling you get that something, somewhere, has gone terribly wrong.

Wadbister: The feeling after having tried to dry one self with a damp towel.

Whirly Knowe: One who dances with no apparent understanding of the music, timing or the steps.

Yaafield: The look on the faces of people who think a boring person has finished speaking when in fact they are only really beginning.

Musical Abilities

I'm one of those hundreds of folk who love music, but cannot play a note. Well, that's not exactly true, as I did at one time in the sixties play the flute, and was of course going to be the next Ian Anderson of Jethro Tull! Having not touched the instrument in over 40 years the chances of me getting a sound out of it now is next to non-existent.

Some fifty years ago there was no Folk Festival or any 'festival' of any sorts bar the annual School Music Festival. This was a musical extravaganza held every year in the Garrison Theatre. A showpiece for the music teachers to show off their protégés and other exciting, talented young pupils – and then there was me. I had been allowed a recorder at some time in the distant past but, after a slow decline through the classier instruments, had been demoted to the triangle. I, however, never saw this as any form of relegation, but just accepted the fact that I was able and allowed to hit metal things with another metal thing and make a sound. I should point out this all took place during my primary school days, in case you thought I was referring to a later senior education period.

The day of the festival dawned and we were all instructed to attend in our best white shirts and grey trousers; the lasses in similar pristine white blouses and grey skirts. Our performance was scheduled last in the order of playing, and as such we would end the festival, prior to the judging. Excitement was in the air. Tension mounted. Socks were continually pulled up. Then there was a small crisis. Somebody, I forget who now, but they were the chief-big-cymbal-player and had taken ill, so a replacement was required. After a lot of discussion it was decided that nobody could be spared from the main instrument line-up, but triangle players were two-a-penny and completely dispensable. So it came to be that young Magnie was destined for his five minutes of fame and glory. He was chosen as the dispensable triangle player. A very quick lesson in cymbal playing ensued, but having already played this – as well as just about every other musical instrument in the 'orchestra' – while I worked my way downwards through the various pieces of apparatus, I was quickly deemed an alternative to Cymbal Man.

The moment arrived and we all trooped on stage, those with their recorders, xylophones, drums, tambourines, triangles, and finally the cymbals. We cymbalists took up position at the back of the orchestra as our moment would come towards the end, in a loud crescendo of clashing metal similar to Tchaikovsky's *1812 Overture*. Only, we were doing some primary school musical thing which sort of pinged and banged and clashed, and Mrs Music Teacher waved a white stick at us and everybody else it seemed. She also seemed to take on quite frightening head-banging sessions and grunted a lot. We, in turn, were to watch and at certain grunts had to blow, ping, bang and clash. Clashing was my forte, and I was all prepared for it.

The noise to my ears was pretty horrendous, but a lot of smiling and nodding Mums obviously approved of their protégés' and little darlings' efforts. I could sense my moment was approaching as Mrs Music kept looking in my direction, and raising her eyebrows and winking. I wasn't too prepared for these pre-clash signals, and nearly blew it as I raised the cymbals apart and was just about to come down with the massive crescendo when she glared with the venom of a rattlesnake... I decided this was not my moment. The racket continued apace and then I sensed it was getting nearer the final countdown because she started twitching a lot and nodding. I drew the cymbals apart and got ready for the exciting up-and-down movement whereby I would lift one cymbal above my head in a vertical position, the second one down between my legs. These I then would bring together in a fast but stylish 'swish' and they would then meet at the precise moment in the music to produce that almighty clash, and I would follow this up with another two 'swishes' and the rest of the troupe would then fade away quietly, instrument by instrument, in a slow but beautiful finale.

The Big Nod came and I 'swished' mightily. I may have been slightly distracted by young Charlie sticking his drum stick up young Michael's backside just in front of me, but as the downward cymbal gathered speed the trajectory moved ever so slightly off course. The edges of these large brass cymbals are quite thin and subsequently quite sharp... as I found out. This circular blade sliced through my thumb at a huge velocity and everything started to happen very quickly then. The blood spurted out at an amazing speed, shot forward and covered young Fiona's blouse from behind. She sort of jumped about a bit – in fact a huge amount – but as I was still concentrating on my now upward stroke, not wanting to miss my golden moment, I tried professionally to ignore her antics. This arm 'swishing' manoeuvre seemed to spread the blood about a bit, so most of the little drummer boys were soon speckled bright red. Fiona, in her startled condition, bumped into the other recorder players who in turn knocked into the triangle men. Things were getting decidedly out of control here, but cymbal man was pressing on with his repertoire having one more downward stroke to finish off his piece. That's when I felt the right-hand cymbal beginning to slip a bit as blood covered the leather hooked thing around my now damaged thumb. The force of my determined swishing resulted in the blessed thing shooting skywards out of my hand and I heard a scream from Mrs Music and a loud "OH, MY GOD!" together with a huge gasp from the audience. Cymbal-less, I couldn't manage my final piece de resistance, so stood and watched the flying cymbal spinning out of control above my head, way up among the curtains and lights. What goes up must come down – unfortunately. Down it came... Well, that sure shifted the orchestra as they all began to run around the stage, bumping into one another in the ensuing panic, till one of them accidentally knocked into Mrs Music and I last saw her disappear backwards over the edge of the stage. Not a pretty sight. The cymbal landed onto the stage in a loud clatter and as I tried to wrap up my hand in my hankie I saw this other disembodied hand appear slowly over the edge of the stage, and finally a very dishevelled Mrs Music's head came into sight.

The orchestra, resplendent in their new red and white costumes, didn't sway the adjudicator. We didn't win, we didn't even come close, in fact we were basically eliminated from the whole festival.

My music career faltered slightly after that. I was never invited to play any instrument in any orchestra, band, ensemble, quartet or duet ever again. Not ever. Shame really, as I thought I showed such potential...

Here, Kitty, Kitty

There are times in life that, no matter how often you have put it off, you have to take your cat to the vet. This procedure should have a government health warning attached to it, and possibly, as appears to be the norm in everything nowadays, a fully detailed risk assessment. I imagine on completion of such a document, this whole cat and vet scenario would rank up there with bomb disposal in the 'probable high injury' stakes. What is it about cats and vets?

Dogs are a different kettle of fish entirely. Any dog we've had over the years never had a problem with vets. All our dogs were a bit loopy right enough, but to them a trip to the vet was considered *"Great! One of my favourite things!"* You put a lead on them, and immediately it was *"Woo-hoo, a walk!"* Then, on arriving at the car, it was *"Woo-hoo, a run in the car. Even better"'* They duly bounced around the back seat, thrashing around from side window to side window, sticking their heads out and letting the wind blow through their ears, while spitting at passing trucks and buses. On arrival at the vets, they were beside themselves with excitement as, on entering the premises, all their dreams had come true as they saw lined up along the wall their idea of heaven – row upon row of cats, contained in small boxes. *"Woo-hoo, take-aways! My favourite thing!"* True, the actual surgery appointment was a bit of a let down, as some green-suited individual shoved a needle in them, but that seemed to pale into insignificance, when weighed up against the huge amount of positives.

Cats, however, view the whole thing as a life threatening disaster of infinite dimensions. I can understand our Elwood's reluctance to go within 1,000 miles of such a practitioner right enough, as when our daughter originally acquired this cat from the Cats Protection League many years ago 'he' was in fact Chloe. Now, he was no transvestite cat, but a small malfunction in the kitten-sexing programme had deemed 'him' to be a 'her'. On his initial visit to the antiseptic smelling rooms he was re-assessed by a rather boorish locum who, in his infinite wisdom, upended Chloe and poked about her in a manner far too forward for a first acquaintance, and declared 'she' a 'he'. That alone was bound to be psychologically traumatic, but he also immediately suggested that a small neutering operation was called for.

We duly collected a very subdued cat the following day, who ambled slowly out of the basket and walked around the sitting room with his rear legs very wide apart for most of the day, giving us numerous 'looks could kill' glances at every opportunity. As a result of that visit it understandably became ingrained in his memory and at the mere mention of the word vet, or even when we spelled it out as V-E-T if he was within earshot, he immediately slid the ears back and the eyes became two huge round black globes. He was on the defensive and we were in for a battle of enormous proportions.

In the early days we wrongly assumed we just had to lift him up and place him in his cat basket where a newly washed rug and his catnip impregnated mouse lay inside. Well, we got that bit wrong... massively wrong. I picked him up and, muttering words of encouragement and endearment, went to slide him in through the open end of the cat basket. He went from being a soft, limp, purring individual into the Hammer House of Horror cat in about three seconds flat. Jeez... he stiffened every limb, muscle, tendon and sinew in his body and adopted the starfish shape. This, if you have never encountered it, is where a cat spreads out each leg as wide as possible, stiffens its tail and flicks out each and every claw to its longest extension. He is now twice the size he was and there is no way he is going to fit inside the door of a normal sized cat basket. In fact, I doubt if he would fit through a standard garage door in this shape. On top of this, he sank every claw into any piece of exposed human skin he saw and drove them in deep to ensure a firm foothold.

At this point I was jumping around the room with a large oversized rug clamped to my body, in mortal agony and some astonishment as well, as Elwood had suddenly turned into a wild raging beast. The next thing I knew he had released his hold on my body and sprung up on top of my head, compressing himself to my scalp. For goodness sake! I scrabbled at the blessed thing and it in turn cloored my hands and forearms before leaping off the top of my head onto the kitchen worktop, cleaning four pans and the cutlery all over the floor. Meanwhile, I was bleeding profusely over everything and the top of my head resembled an old pin cushion full of holes. Dear God, for such a mess! What the hell's possessed the thing?

"I don't think he wants to go to the vet!"

Well, I think I gathered that! There now followed a hunt and destroy mission which began to take on machinations of military proportions.

"Here, kitty, kitty!"

"Where the hell is he now?"

I had noticed him briefly (while I was having my lacerated, punctured limbs and body attended to by the 'paramedics') climbing up the curtains in the sitting room, but he appears to have moved on from that as they are now lying all askew, some having been flipped off the hooks. I adopted a new tactic in so much that I armed myself with a large bath towel, the idea being that should I come within a few feet or so of the beast I could possibly wrap him up quietly and comfortably in it.

After about half an hour, I had finally located the feline answer to Dracula, underneath the bed in the spare room. As far underneath the bed as it is possible to be. There was nothing else for it, I just had to crawl in after him. In an admirably heroic strategic move, I closed the bedroom door, so blocking any means of escape, and now got down on all fours and started my Goose Green approach. Arm by arm I got nearer, and in the distant darkness two large round green and black eyes watched my struggling efforts to approach them. Just as I thought I might manage to grab an outlying paw, he spat, and in a flash dived straight at my head. I ducked quickly and just managed to crack my forehead on the floor as he sprinted over the top of my receding hairline, giving it a quick couple of deep scratches just for good measure in the process. He's now out from under the bed and I too make a swift exit, scrambling back rearwards out into the room again, smacking my head yet again off the wooden slats underneath the bed.

Eventually I emerge determined to catch the little beggar if it's the last thing I do – and it may well be. There then follows a chase around the bedroom, where I leap about liked a demented frog, bouncing off the top of the bed as I chase him over and around everything in sight. At last he stops to watch as I sit down on the bed gasping for air, bleeding and battered, and suddenly I see a moment when, coolly thinking he's outfoxed me once again, he calmly starts to clean his face, his gaze averted. The moment is not to be missed. I launch myself off the bed and, in a rugby tackle of Jonah Lomu standards, fly through the air with the towel outstretched, and while it all seems to happen in desperately slow motion, I land on top of an unsuspecting cat and wrap him up tightly in the towel. He squirms violently inside but I hold on even though the claws are starting to pierce through the thick fluffiness of the towel. I grasp him grimly and tightly, then suddenly a very mad cat's head appears from underneath the towel. He glares at me violently, death is in his mind, but with the towel tightly wrapped around him I transport him down the stairs and unceremoniously dump him headfirst into the cat basket and shut the cage door front. Success! Moderated somewhat by the trail of blood and destruction left in his wake.

Of course, after all this he sits in the box humming a little tune all the way to the vet, steps smartly out of the basket, nudges her arm, purring sweetly while fluttering his eyelashes, and afterwards swaggers back into the basket with not so much as a murmur.

This is unreal. I have to go through this whole performance at least once a year to give him his booster vaccination. Still, this little episode is nothing compared to the process of giving a him a tablet...you definitely don't want to go there... not ever.

Snow Crisis...

I quite like snow, I am a snow person, much more so than wind and rain and suchlike. Snow probably comes up there near the top along with sun and sunrises and sunsets and clouds and calm days. The thing with snow is it tends to cause a certain amount of disruption and, in my case, occasionally complete mayhem in my life. This is not altogether bad, but does tend to upset things slightly.

Last year it snowed a lot, and coupled with the wind it resulted in the road down to our house being fanned up with the drifting snow. This meant that even the old trusty Subaru couldn't make it either up or down the road, so I had to leave her at the top of the road and venture down on foot. The only problem was I had loaded up the car with the week's 'Big Shop' from Tesco, as well as 10 bags of hardwood logs to keep the home fires burning.

However, I hit on a plan which I had used before, and after a rummage around in the garage I got out 'my' trusty red plastic sledge. As Elwood the cat was sitting watching my every move, I did at one point discuss with him the possibility of a harness attachment and showed him the picture of Shackleton the Explorer Cat, whose exploits I related in some detail. He sat and listened, though I could tell he was bored as his eyes kept going together and his head drooped, and only when I prodded him and shook the straps did he give me 'The Stare' and I fully realised then that this was not going to happen. Not in a million years. He stalked off out the door and as I followed and trundled up the hill, pulling the sledge behind me, he fell in line and bounced from each snow hole to the next, following me all the way to the top of the road and the car. I guess he knew there was going to be some sport in this venture and he was making doubly sure he didn't miss it.

On arrival at the car, I decided that I would load up the Tesco bags first and get supplies down to the house initially, and leave the bags of logs till last. I got the first two bags positioned well on the sledge and, to make the whole process more exciting, I decided that I would sit at the rear and enjoy a sledge down the hill at the same time. I shuffled along on the sledge till I got to the top of the slope and, positioning the bows of the sledge in line with the far away garage door, I launched myself off and down the slope.

A couple of seconds later, as I tried desperately to extract my head and arms from the fencing wire, I watched as a bright green lettuce disappeared over the brow of the hill and was lost in the deeper snow. Things had not gone well at the start. I had pushed a bit too fiercely with my right leg resulting in a violent lurch to the left, straight into the fence, and me and the two Tesco bags had shot forward and, thankfully, brought up very quickly in the fencing wire... there is a 30-foot drop on the other side. Elwood had not budged from his vantage point at the top of the road, and he was sitting there shaking his head in disbelief.

Another couple of minutes passed while I shuffled back to the centre of the road and got things lined up once more. A big heave and away we go this time... swooosh... down the slope and gathering speed all the time; the snow was crisp and shiny, perfect for sledging and things were going well... then we hit the big fan of snow on the left hand side. I was intending to skirt this but, not seeing too well over the shopping bags, I misjudged the approach and we took on a list not unlike the style you see in a luge race in the Winter Olympics. We were now speeding down at an ever-increasing velocity, at a jaunty 45-degree angle, as we ploughed through the deep fan of snow. I now had to hold on desperately to the heavy bags and this speed of descent was also resulting in some of the contents spilling out – a couple of tins of beans and a selection of green apples and bananas overtook me on the right. Things started to get a bit more out of hand as we hurtled downhill at breakneck speed... the angle had increased as we took a higher line through the fan of snow... it had risen to nearer 60-degrees and was tilting higher. How these bobsleigh guys can hang on in there is a mystery to me... two Tesco bags and I were having a serious job trying to stay upright.

The next few seconds were over in a flash, and I don't really know what actually happened, but I was aware of a bag of potatoes smacking me around the head as I shot out of the sledge, clutching the shopping tightly to my chest. I ploughed into the soft fan of snow headfirst and disappeared momentarily before re-emerging in a burst of white crystals as I slammed into the wire fence once again. I lay there on my back with the bags beside me. I looked up to a dark, clear blue sky with the stars twinkling above me and began to wonder just where the hell I was. Then reality stepped in and, worryingly, I began to feel the sensation of a weight on my legs, then my stomach, and finally a tickling sensation in my face. I was sure now that some serious damage had been done and I was slowly losing the feeling throughout my body. I looked up to check if my legs still lay in the right position... straight into the face of Elwood. He in turn was standing on my chest and giving me the once over, satisfied I was still alive and, while not necessarily well, would still be able to open a packet of Senior Whiskas.

Dear God, that was a bit close... now I clambered up and looked for the sledge. There it was, away down at the bottom of the slope, minus both me and the bags. I gathered up the food and popped it all back in the bags, bar the lettuce and a can of coconut milk which I never saw again. I then sauntered casually down to collect the sledge, in case anybody had seen my antics, and to appear nonchalant and able to deal with potential disasters in a controlled manner. The fact that I had a large bunch of fresh coriander festooned across my woolly hat may have conveyed things differently (but I was not to know about that until I finally made it to the house and was questioned on my choice of fascinator).

Elwood was now sitting about a foot or so away from me, staring at this apparition that stood before him... and you could see his mind slowly turning over... *"You're nuts... you really are..."*

It's Curtains For All of Us

Sometimes I think shopping is a penance delivered down to us males of the species by a revengeful superior being. The females of this world by-and-large enjoy this activity, though some purport not to and try to hoodwink us into thinking they are like us. Not true. Nobody has the trials and tribulations that we men do when we undertake to go shopping for some little clothing purchase. I – and this is a personal account of things – tend to use the blitz approach, whereby I head for the nearest store, do a five- or ten-minute recce, see the item I need, pick it up, march to the sales counter, pay for it, bag it and walk away. End of story.

Some lady buyers, however, seem to use the stealth approach. They overfly a huge number of shops, find the very item they want, pick it up, look at it, turn it round, put it back on the rail, go away, come back to it, pick it up, look at it, turn it round, put it back on the rail, and go away; maybe even leave the store altogether. They do the same procedure in a huge number of shops, eventually to return to the first one to discover the size they wanted has now gone, and so the whole process starts again to find a suitable alternative. I cannot quite figure that out, but apparently it's all to do with choice and maybe, just maybe, out there somewhere is a better bargain that, if discovered after purchasing the first choice, would be a disaster of cataclysmic proportions.

Okay, I can see some logic in this, but the trauma of having to go through the 'ultimate shopping horror' over and over again just appals me, and I couldn't cope with that. This ultimate shopping horror is, of course, the dreaded 'trying it on' process. I really detest this part of shopping, and can very happily purchase socks, underwear, shirts in general, casual or otherwise, but trousers... I begin to break out in a cold sweat and start to shake violently at the very thought of it. It brings back far, far too many disastrous memories of moments of sheer and utter bedlam that have befallen me over the years.

The first approach to buying trousers, be they smart dress ones or simply casual jeans or chinos, is to go and weigh up the choices. Not one shop has the same size in all their trousers; I know from experience that this is the truth. Each shop, though it may like to think there is a universal sizing regime in place, is just kidding itself. Trousers are all made by some little tailor in some far off country and his selection of sizes differs greatly from his pal in another far off country. A size 36 waist in one is a size 34, or even a size 38, in another. A leg length of 34 in one is a 32 in another, and so on it goes. This means that I have to 'try them on'. A relatively simple process, that hundreds of men are capable of doing day in day out. Why, then, do you think it causes me so much grief and distress? Is it me... or is it that there is some kind of hidden force-field surrounding those horror chambers they call 'Fitting Rooms'?

I generally find, after a long time of looking and wondering and holding them up alongside me, that I finally have the strength to take two, or even maybe three pairs to the 'Fitting Rooms' and I stride off in search of an assistant. Within seconds of my approach towards these little cubicles, there appears three or more of these people, each one eager to help and 'assist'. I faff about with my prospective purchase and she leads me off and into the inner sanctum, and guides me through the opening, and there before me is a choice of three small cupboards with a sliding curtain concealing the entrance. This she sweeps aside in a confident manner, and ushers me through with the now familiar words... *"There you go, sir, and just give me a shout if you need any assistance."*

I am now inside this 'room', which if I'm lucky is about three feet square with a chair in one corner taking up most of the floor space and a large mirror on the opposite wall. This mirror is almost always at least one human head length too low. I look across at it and can see myself from the neck and down to my ankles. There are no head and no feet visible. I try to stand back a bit to see if the view improves, but it doesn't really. I then try the one foot forward and one foot back approach, where I am standing like some Robin Hood archer ready to shoot off a whole quiver of arrows. This stance does allow for one foot and a fair section of my head to be seen. I lower myself a few inches more and there, I can see most of my long body in the mirror now. Just then, the curtain swings back and the assistant pokes her head in, and sees me in this squatting position, still dressed as I went into the cubicle. She gives me a long hard look before uttering, *"I'm just awa fir ma tea, so if you're needing ony help then Rita will be here for you."*

Then, after a long pause as she holds the curtain back so Rita can also see my unusual position, she leans a bit farther in and says, *"Yer aaricht, aren't ye... yer nae haeing a seizure are ye?"*

"No, no," says I, *"I was just about to get changed."*

"Aye... ah weel, as lang as yer sure yer nae haein a seizure, as wir nae wantin nane o' that kerry on in here."

"No, no, I'm fine."

Good job I hadn't just whipped off my trousers at that point, as Rita's colleague was still holding the curtains wide open so everybody in the store could see and hear the 'victim' inside. Finally, she let it slip and I started to change and took off my jacket. Now, why is it there is only one silly little hook on the wall here. You would think they might have thought *"Heh, these guys are going to take off jackets, trousers, shirts maybe, so let's give them a few hooks and a couple of hangers..."* But no, one paltry hook, that's it! Onto the hook goes my outside jacket, and then I sit down and start to get the trousers off. By this time I'm pretty fed up of all this de-robing in a cupboard the size of a cigarette packet. I've already banged my head and elbow on the opposing walls and am a tad annoyed, so decide that, basically, stuff it, I'm just going to pull the trousers off over my shoes as I just can't be bothered to untie and retie my shoes over and over again.

Most times, I can generally slip the trouser leg off over a shoe no problem, but go inside a 'fitting room' and everything takes on an air of total disaster. I successfully manage to get one leg off, and am on the second leg when the trouser bottom jams over the heel of the shoe and I'm left hopping about the cupboard on one leg while trying to pull the errant leg off the shoe. I start to hop slightly more violently as I pull ever harder on the offending trouser leg. This sets in motion a series of events that neither Marks & Spencer nor Rita and a few others are ever really ready for.

As I bounce around inside the room I can feel my balance going, and as I am now in a position with my trousers around my ankles, one leg flapping freely while the other one impedes my forward progress somewhat, I lurch towards the wall. I'm still holding onto the trapped leg, so stick out my free hand to balance myself on the solid wall. Unfortunately, I misjudge the actual wall position and instead of connecting with it I shoot past and my hand goes through the curtained opening, resulting in me being propelled even faster forward. Grabbing desperately at the curtain, I manage to secure a grip on it to try and steady myself but, as I've made rather a fierce lunge, I inadvertently pull the curtain from the rings securing it to the upper rail... me, the curtain, and my trousers, shoot out through the opening and land headfirst at the feet of a small Aberdeen woman who is sitting waiting patiently for her husband to emerge from the fitting room.

This gives her a pretty nasty scare, as you can imagine. Sitting there minding her own business, suddenly there's a 6ft-plus guy who leaps out of a cubicle with no trousers on and attacks her. I think possibly if she hadn't jumped up so quickly, things might have been calmer, but she shrieked loudly and on rising tripped over her chair and fell on top of me. At this point her husband stepped outside his cubicle wearing what I can only describe as a lurid deep red jacket (I think both of them must have been a trifle colour blind), but he was met with the scene of his wife of many years cavorting around the floor of Marks & Spencer with another man wearing no trousers.

Rita was beside herself, and summoned a whole host of

substitute assistants who had been sitting on the bench seemingly awaiting just such an event, as within minutes I was surrounded by around six or seven of them, all trying to lift Mrs Aberdeen up off the top of me. Meanwhile, Mr Flamingo ran around the sorry mess in a state of fear and alarm, trying to tell everybody that Mrs Aberdeen had never done this sort of thing before.

I finally managed to get myself extricated from the heap and hauled up one leg of the trousers, plus the offending leg itself, and so there was a modicum of decorum at last. I gave my apologies to Elsie, as Mrs Aberdeen was called, and she was re-seated and tea was brought to calm the whole sorry situation down. I tried to explain what had happened and, to be honest, she was a sprightly little soul and having now got over the initial fright began to see the funny side.

Mr Flamingo, or Maurice as he was known, still wasn't quite sure who had instigated the raucous behaviour and so stood a bit back from the scene, before finally taking up position in front of me and directly in front of Elsie and enquiring of her, *"Well, after all that... what do you think?"*

Elsie looked up at him, looked across at me, and then turned and said, *"No, Maurice, no I don't think pink's your colour really."*

I got my shoes off, pulled up my trousers, stood on a chair and re-hooked the curtains to the rings, tidied up the mess and put my clothes all back on again, before finally seeing that Elsie was okay. Then I said my goodbyes.

As I left the fitting rooms, Rita, the super-assistant, called after me, *"Are ye nae wanting tae try on anither pair then...?"*

I looked back and saw a line-up of M&S assistants all grinning like a row of Cheshire Cats, waving two pairs of trousers at me...

Homeward Bound

Our holiday over with and after the usual rugby scrum that is the flight check-in, an hour or so later we boarded the flight back to Scotland. Once again we had a very pleasant journey and sampled the menu being proffered by Sharlene, the attendant, as she sweetly shouted above the engine noise, *"Is you'se wantin' a panini or one o' they coronation chickens? They're the berries, so they are."*

This time I chose a coronation chicken sandwich and, while maybe I wouldn't have said it was fantastic, it was fresh, tasty, and washed down with a small bottle of vino tinto was quite refreshing. It was made even more so while I watched the couples who bring their picnics on cheap flights, munching their way through dry Pringles, cling-film-wrapped sandwiches stuffed with limp lettuce, and bottles of lukewarm water with bits floating in it.

Then it was into Waverley Station and off to catch the train to Aberdeen. Is it the Mediterranean diet, do they just take more care of their bodies, or is it something to do with the climate... during our 10 days abroad I could probably count on one hand the number of obese people we saw, but within half an hour at Waverley I lost count of the numbers who waddled past us. Possibly the fact we were sitting right outside Burger King may have had something to do with it, as it obviously attracts the large of the species that seem inextricably drawn to its delights, like bees around a honey pot.

Onto the 'Crosscountry' train and woo-hoo... what's going on here! The whole train is packed to the gunwales with a collection of assorted Scottish people heading north after a weekend in the capital. Everyone seems to have a case the size of Africa, plus their entire food intake for a week stacked around them and jammed in to every available space. We battle our way down the carriage, trailing our meagre cases behind us – no room in the luggage compartments while the entire contents of IKEA, Primark and M&S are stowed there.

We arrive at our 'reserved' seats to find a young lad opportunistically occupying our pew... no hassle, a quick discussion on tickets and he's on his way to poach one somewhere else. Meanwhile, we pack one case in between the seats and one in the aisle, my good wife clambers in on top and has to lie across them and me, while I squash into the second seat and balance the aisle case, my legs and arms in the alleyway. So much for the advert emblazoned along the sides of the maroon and grey carriages... *"How can we make sure you arrive fresh, not frazzled?"* Hah!

At least we have a seat. Seven guys who joined in Darlington, and have obviously been enjoying the hospitality suite, are attempting to stand, there being no unreserved seats available. They don't seem to mind and entertain us with renditions of various songs. A conductor-type person emerges and asks them for their tickets, a session of gay and merry banter ensues as they all attempt to locate the tickets. One guy falls over, but emerges from the melee of legs and arms with his ticket held high. She tells them to go and try another carriage as there may be seats available there. On they go, singing a selection from 'Snow White and the Seven Dwarfs'... *"Heigh ho, heigh ho"*... combined with the yodelling one *"Ho-la-la-ee-ay, Ho-la-la-ee-ay"*. I'll miss them, they brightened up the journey.

We shunt on to various small towns heading north and more people seem to get on with very few disembarking. Things are getting serious now. My legs and one arm have gone to sleep. I hope nobody asks me to get up as I would imagine any attempt at forward movement will render me a crumpled mess on the floor.

I haul my case towards me as a few more passengers embark at Kinross, among them a tall, leggy, dark-haired model look-alike who sits down opposite me. She's attractive in a Next catalogue stick insect sort of way, with a massive yellow designer handbag and a pink overhead-luggage case. She settles down and out comes the sparkling mobile phone. Why do folks always have to phone as soon as they get on a train to tell somebody they are on a train? I don't get it.

She obviously wants us all to hear her. Talks loudly: *"Oh, hello darling, it's me... yes, I'm on the train to Aberdeen..."* (Whoopee!)

"Ooooo, it's just packed..." (No kidding!)

"Yes, yes, all types... and the rest..." (Well hello, dear!)

"I know, I know, and wasn't Cannes just WONDERFUL!" (Here we go!)

"Yes, and Rhuraidh was such a hoot in Monte Carlo..." (Good for Rhuraidh!)

"Is it Miami this weekend or are you going skiing in Montenegro instead?" (Aaarghh!)

After a good few minutes of this – and we've name-dropped a few exciting places along with a few others I wouldn't be seen dead in – she flutters the eyelashes at her audience, folds up the phone and sits still.

Now it's my turn. I set my phone to test ring and, feigning surprise, take it out of my jacket, smiling at her apologetically... talk loudly: *"Hello... Hello... Oh, hi Barack, how's it going? Good, good... and Michelle and the girls? Okay, that's magic. Yes, no problem, will do, I'll send on a vacuum pack as soon as I get home. Yes, yes, speak soon... take care, all the best, cheers."*

As I put the phone away, she's staring at me... I shake the head... *"Obama... some guy, loves his saucermeat."*

Not long after, she moves seats, still giving me a long hard look. Maybe it was the phone call, or possibly the twitching in my right leg as the feeling started to return and it sort of jumped around a bit. Whatever.

As we approach Dundee, the conductor breezes through the carriage herding the seven lads from Darlington ahead of her.

"Right, well you just get off here at Dundee, and there is another train just 20 minutes behind this with plenty seats and you can get on that one."

The lads disembark and light up on the platform while awaiting the next train. A few more folks get on, and even with the Magnificent Seven now ashore there are no more seats available and my fellow traveller still has to lie across the seats and the cases. She's beginning to get a cramp and is none too excited about UK train travel at the moment. We slowly move out and faintly in the distance as we trundle out of the station I can hear the strains of *"Farewell, farewell, it's time for us to go-ho..."* The Darlington boys have moved on to the 'Sound of Music' now.

The rest of the journey passes without incident, no more seats become available and we make it to Aberdeen, haul our cases out onto the platform, try and straighten up, shuffle down towards the exit as the feeling starts to come back into our nether regions, legs and arms, and make our way out to the waiting taxis. There are a few lined up so we join the queue and hop into a black cab type vehicle with no visible markings and ask to be taken to the Express by Holiday Inn on Chapel Street. He clicks the meter and away we go, out onto Guild Street and around up onto Union Street. We're relaxed now; we will get our cases into the room, freshen up, and head out to La Tasca for a Spanish tapas meal to round off the holiday.

Peeeep! Peeeep!

"What the hell are you playing at...? You dozy doughball!"

Dear God, we're nearly catapulted off the back seat onto the floor, as he brakes violently and swerves to avoid a young guy in a white souped-up Nissan who cuts in front of him at the lights.

"Mirrrrror. Signaaaal. Manooooverrrrr! Mirrrrror. Signaaaal. Manooooverrrrr!"

Our driver is now leaning out the window, driving right up behind this young lad, roaring instructions out at him. He in turn is leaning out of his window, looking backwards, replying with a selection of choice Aberdonian phrases, most of which shed some doubt on our driver's parental status.

We are then subjected to a tirade on the driving habits of Aberdonians in general, young drivers, his own driving standards, the driving test, the basic principle of 'mirror-signal-manoeuvre', that he learned about 40 years ago, and a lot more bedsides. Thankfully, our hotel is just round the corner and we screech to a halt outside the door. He's out of the cab like a bullet, still remonstrating loudly to all who will listen, and as he hands me our cases, I manage to get a word in and confirm the cost of our taxi. I settle up and he's away to the driver's seat again, in the cab, and off.

Well, that was an experience!

Heh, hold on a minute, where's my other case, my trusty rucksack? Oh, for goodness sake, he's driven off with it! Off we go into the hotel, and explain our problem.

"What was the name of the cab, sir?... Rainbow?"

"No, I don't think so... didn't seem to have any name on it."

"Central, maybe?"

"No, not sure."

"Don Cabs?"

"Uh... huh."

"City? Ace...? Was there anything of importance or value in your bag, sir?"

"Well, all my heart tablets, our passports, train, boat and plane tickets... but no money or credit cards," I add brightly.

"Think we had better call the Aberdeen Police Lost Property Office to report it first off."

"Yes, ok." Seems like a good idea.

"Now, sir, can you describe the tablets you've lost?"

I list all my various assorted prescription tablets.

"Ok, I see, sir, that seems quite a lot... are there any of them... what we might call... eh... dangerous?"

"Dangerous?"

"Ah, yes, sir... how can I say this... eh... is there any Valium or Diazepam etc?"

"No, but I could do with some right now, ha ha!"

"Yes, quite, sir... okay, we will advise you if it gets handed in."

Very friendly and helpful, but I somehow doubt it's ever going to be handed in as such; we need to try a more direct approach here.

Just then Big Kenny arrives on the scene. He's one of the reception staff at the hotel, and he springs into action. We relate our story again and he seems to know every taxi firm in Aberdeen and all the call centre staff. He phones around, and then tells me he's left word with them all and they have agreed to broadcast the message on air, so all the drivers will hear it and hopefully one of them might be a 55-year-old, grey-haired, small Aberdonian with a short fuse.

We go to our room, unable to settle really until we hear any word. I venture outside and wander down to the taxi rank at the foot of Chapel Street to chat to the drivers there to see if any of them recognise our guy.

"About 55 you say, grey hair, short... aye... weel that fairly narrows it doon son... there are joost aboot 5,000 o' wis lik that!"

An hour or so later, reception calls to say that Mr Mirror-Signal-Manoeuvre has been and handed in the bag. Magic. Didn't actually expect that to happen but, thanks to Big Kenny and the rest of the Express by Holiday Inn staff, he was tracked down. Well done.

Off out we go to try and get a tapas or two before bed. We end up with a fish supper, from a Polish woman in a side street near the hotel, which was a big mistake. Sunday fish suppers anywhere is a bad idea, with the last markets on a Friday morning, but in Aberdeen they are seriously bad. But never mind, I've got my rucksack, my heart tablets and our NorthLink ticket, and we'll get some good freshly cooked haddock and chips onboard there. Mmmm...

Sport For All

Now, I am not exactly a huge sports fanatic. Football, swimming, basketball, golf, tennis, sailing – I can watch these when there's not a lot of other stuff on the TV. I have also participated in all of them with varying degrees of success. It's not that I am completely useless at sport, but I have a certain tendency for sport not to be my best friend at times.

Take football for instance. I grew up with three-a-side, or five-a-side, or however-many-a-side turned up, and the rules were very loose. Really very loose. The goalposts were generally two guys' jackets or jumpers, and the goals themselves were the back of the old school huts or somebody's metal garage door, and there was always only one set of goals. Some clever arrangement ensued that there was a 'score' at the end. These always assumed that the owner of the garage door didn't come out and chase you away from what was very probably, by now, a slightly dented garage door.

From this we progressed to after-school kick-abouts, and then onto the Anderson Educational Institute, or to give its more modern title the Anderson High School. This entitled you to play a game of interesting football on the then sloping field at Bellevue. I was picked for an AEI team purely on the basis that I could run fast, not necessarily with the ball, but I could cover the ground at a fair old speed. This, therefore, decided my position and I was duly placed on the outside right. Nobody took into consideration that I didn't see too well with my left eye, so much so that I continually had to run forward with my head turned at ninety degrees to the direction I was heading in, just to try and keep a check on the rest of the field. This was okay when I was attempting, in my lumbering way, to keep pace with the play, but a right nuisance really when somebody foolishly passed the ball to me.

On one such occasion, I had been running up and down the touchline looking as if I knew what I was doing, when suddenly the ball landed at my feet. I set off down the wing at some speed and was aware that I was well ahead of the opposition and glanced across to see the rest of my team waving and gesticulating frantically at me. I checked the goal ahead and was just about to launch a belter of a shot, when I seemed to recognise the guy in the goals. He was our own team's goalie. In my excitement at getting the ball, I had set off in the wrong direction! However, a deft sleight of foot, and I was soon heading back down the wing again and gathering speed towards the correct goal. Amazingly, I dribbled past a couple of players before it dawned on me they were our guys again, and I didn't really need to swerve and cut across them, but I carried on in my stylish way.

I was aware of a lot of shouting again on my left hand side, but desperate not to lose the ball by having to turn my head round and look across, I ploughed on. Just then I was briefly aware of a thundering sound and a huge shadow overcame me and, in an instant, I was bundled off the ball and literally flew through the air, landing outside the touchline in a heap of legs and arms, rolling over a couple of times before finally coming to rest on my back. This was no Italian theatricals, this was the real McCoy!

I had no idea what had hit me, but assumed it must have been a wayward truck or some such thing, as I could hardly feel anything from the neck and down. My legs appeared to be lying at a very funny angle, but after a minute or so I managed to unravel them and was happy to see both my feet seemed to be pointing in the same direction. The game had continued and, as these were the days of allowable shoulder charges, I had obviously been the recipient of a legitimate tackle as there was no whistle blowing, or free kicks being given. In fact, I was basically lying there and the team were playing with 10 men. The eleventh was clearly not worth bothering about, and I'm sure some thought the team were a whole lot better without their speedy right winger.

Meanwhile, I tried to extricate myself from the clump of stingy nettles I was now ensconced in. I rolled over and was slowly pulling myself up onto my knees when I felt a hot sweet waft of steamy air surround my head. I looked up, straight into the nostrils of a large black and white cow. Bellevue, at this time, shared the football pitch with somebody's prize heifers. They wandered about outside the pitch and devoured and chewed up the long grass that encircled the ground.

Now, being a Lerwick 'toonie' I was not all that familiar with the bovine world and, while I had seen plenty of them in and around my relations' crofts in Sandwick, I had never really had much cause to share the same airspace as a 1000lb beast breathing heavily into my face from around three inches. I quickly sized up the situation as verging on the dangerous, as she moved in for the kill, and then gave me a huge, large, wet slobbery 'kiss' from the base of my chin right up and over my head. The smell was foul.

I crawled forward and saw the fence straight ahead of me. My saviour. I just had to get to the other side of this and I would be safe. I lurched forward and, to help propel me through and under the wire, I grabbed hold of it and went to pull my battered body through to the other side. What happened next can only be described as electrifying. I started to sort of pulsate and twitch quite violently and couldn't seem to let go of the thin length of wire. I pulled myself up to try and get more leverage on my now quite sore and burning hot hand, but that seemed to start an even more exciting and violent dance. I was now leaping about the edge of the pitch attached to this bloody wire, and out of the corner of my eye I could see the game come to a standstill, as the remaining 21 players on the pitch watched my antics.

Somebody, probably the referee, shouted across to me to stop fooling about and get back on the pitch. I replied that I would if I could. Just then my bovine companion, who had been standing wide eyed with her mouth hanging open, swishing her tail loudly back and fore, decided enough was enough and it was time to take things into her own hands. She backed off a few yards, turned, and loped towards me. With one glancing blow she butted me over the single strand of the electric fence and back onto the pitch. I landed on my back once more, and was promptly trampled on again as the rest of the team charged after the ball and up the wing. I staggered to my feet, and was nursing a sore hand and trying to come to terms with what had just happened, when the ball smacked me between the eyes and ricocheted off over the opposition to land directly in front of our top scorer. He deftly side-footed it around the remaining defender, and nut-megged the on-rushing goalie to score a cracker of a goal... and as it turned out the winning one too.

He was hailed a hero as the rest of the team gathered round and clapped him on the back and punched the air. No hugging and kissing then-a-days. Nobody came to me and thanked me for my powerful headed cross placed so accurately at his feet, though the referee did come up and ask me what the hell I thought I had been doing, dancing with the cows. I think I said I was shocked at what had happened, and cast a glance towards my new bovine 'friend'. She just stood there, jaws swaying back and fore, shook her head and trundled off to join the rest of the herd and tell them how she helped clinch the game for the AEI team...

The other sports I listed at the beginning also seemed to have occasional moments of high drama in them. Basketball after a session of being introduced to Unst home brew, where we then went on to slaughter an RAF team – ostensibly the best in the force – the morning after the night before. Sailing in ballasted boats, when both me and the ballast disappeared over the side in a highly-competitive gybing movement, which cost us the race and very nearly my life, not through drowning, but due to the fact that the skipper's prized lead weights were now very much at the bottom of the ocean. Golf in the heady days of the Sumburgh course, where you had to wait till the planes had landed, and you could get an amazing carry by bouncing the ball across the tarmac of the runways.

The list is probably endless and, as I say, while I took part in many sports, none of them ever became my forte. Though I must say, I had a lot of fun, even if I was damaged for life and have never really trusted cows since.

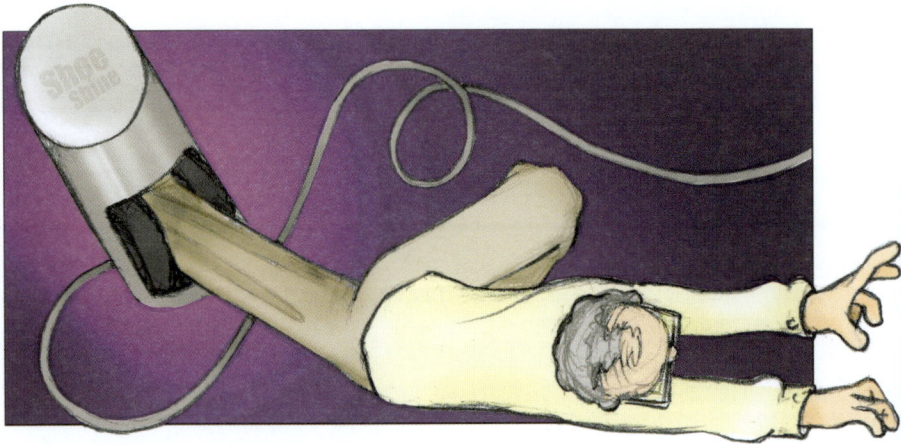

Hotel Aerobics

Over the years I have frequented a number of hotels and other accommodation establishments of varying quality, as I travelled around the UK and Europe, mostly on business but also occasionally on holiday. The thing with business travel is that invariably you are spending the night on your own, as being a traveller from Shetland you have to fly down the night before for a meeting the next day. This arrangement, apart from being costly, ensures a night in a strange town or city and the chance to try out some new hotel facilities.

Things have improved somewhat over the years from the early seventies, in that now nearly every hotel room has a colour TV and a coffee machine with a few assorted small pieces of chipboard wrapped up in some infuriatingly tight plastic, and an assortment of smelly stuff in the bathroom.

On being shown to my hotel room I often partake in a sort of hotel aerobics session where I attempt to see if I can swing from the bathroom door and land on the bed. This determines the size of the room for me. Then I spend a happy hour trying out the TV remote controls. None of these are ever the same – just how many different types of remotes are there in the world? I generally flick through every channel I can find just to see what's on offer, including the radio channels which are often the best anyway. I bypass the 'Hotel Wonderful Welcomes Mr Shearer' page, but use this as a marker for the rest. Why would we all want to watch the *CNN* news channel twenty-four hours a day? But there's no *CBeebies* on offer! I get withdrawal symptoms if I cannot see *Charlie and Lola* at least once when I'm away, and start to twitch a lot if I've missed *Big and Small* after two days.

Once I've established the TV operations and given up all hope of setting the radio alarm, instead now relying on the wonders of the mobile phone to wake me in the morning, I set about the drawers of the various cabinets placed around the room. This, I actually think, is in the forlorn hope somebody has left something exciting in one of them which the cleaners have missed, but apart from the odd sock and a torn copy of Sherlock Holmes in *Hound of the Baskervilles* I've rarely found anything worth keeping. There was one occasion when I came across a small tambourine tucked away in the back of a drawer, and while I had a lot of fun cavorting around the room while tuned into the *MTV* channel that night, I reluctantly put it back in its place rather than take it home. I had this vision of marching through airport security with my hand luggage tinkling merrily and some over zealous officer drawing me to the side while announcing to all around on the tannoy... *"Jim to security please, Jim to security please, we've got a flower-power hippie here with bells on his toes needs checking out."*

Then you need to try out the bed and search for the hidden pillows. This is a cute game all hotels seem to play with me. I like two pillows, good for propping up at night to read with and, also, I just happen to think one thin white effort the thickness of a cream cracker is no way to spend the night. But, try finding where they've hidden the extra pillow. It's a nightmare. I start in the wardrobes – often they have them tucked way in at the back of the top shelf above the coat-racks – but, again, they might be underneath the bed in a sealed plastic bag. Sometimes if it's a large bathroom they handily hide them along with the extra towels. Then again, I have found them in a drawer under the computer-style desk that now seems to inhabit every hotel room. The list is endless, but I cannot settle till I've found them, otherwise it's a call to reception and room service to get my second pillow.

After all that, as many an oft-times-travelled lonesome guest does, I lay out my next day's clothes on the bed with great precision before tidying them away on the hangers provided, leaving something smart but casual for the night ahead. There is no need for this, you can just live out of the suitcase or backpack and forget the 'hanging up' procedure, but for some reason, which I know not, this routine is essential to come to terms with life in a new city, albeit for only a few hours.

If you've spent a day travelling then a shower and a fresh shift of clothes is a must, and here the fun begins. Once more, there must be a hundred, maybe a thousand different shower controls, each one designed to fool you at the least, and possibly maim or scald you at the worst. In some hotels they have kindly left a small plaque on the wall next to the controls, explaining the procedure required to get water out of the shower-rose at the correct temperature and force needed to wash a human. This they have written in letters so small that you need a magnifying glass to read it, and in my case is next to useless. I am in there, standing in the buff, all ready to push, pull, press, twist, turn, or whatever it takes to make it work, but after a few futile attempts whereby the toilet has flushed four times, the tap has spewed out freezing cold water at a hundred miles per hour, and the shower head has fired a couple of rounds of needles into my head, I am no nearer having a shower than winning the lottery.

Eventually I give in and step outside again, back through to find my glasses, back into the shower, bend down and peer at the instructions, check the controls, pull and push a few levers and, after a minute or two, things happen and warmish water envelopes me, and my glasses. I then take them off, slide around on the shower floor and have to step outside again to put them back on the sink. Back into the shower for the third time, grasping a couple of small bottles of shampoo and body wash which never seem to be able to build up a proper lather. I finally emerge smelling sweetly of lavender and vanilla or some such thing.

It's a bit disconcerting to have a bathroom lined with mirrored walls, I must say. In all the years of your life you have never had the occasion to view yourself from behind, side on, or from above all at the same time – and to be honest it's a tad worrying when you actually do. You only then begin to realise what a misshapen object you truly are. Oversized, protruding ears, kinked nose, slightly hairy in places you never realised, and a tad shuffly when you move. It's not a pretty sight and I personally think they should revert to the old days when you just got a round shaving mirror, stuck on the end of an expanding frame, as your only means of identification.

Anyway, after a spell of drying oneself in a thing the size of a postage stamp, you finally pull all the towels out of that fencing-wire frame stuck up on the wall and locate the bath towel, which is of course the opposite in size and roughly the equivalent to a football field. Having stood on all the bits of it while you dry your hair and body, tripped up at least once and smacked yourself into the mirrored cabinet, or in some cases the mirrored wall, you at last get dressed again, ready to face the dining room.

Off down to the dining room, which in a new hotel is sometimes a scary moment as you enter the waiters' hallowed hall of terror. In most cases you tend to dine early in a vain attempt to convince yourself that having eaten a sumptuous meal you will hit town and take the place apart, revelling in many hostelries and nightclubs where you will make friends and influence people. The truth, of course, is completely different. You hover at the sign loudly marked 'Wait here to be allocated a table' or some such similar unfriendly greeting. The dining room is virtually empty, but they keep you hovering around like a lost puppy for ages, before arriving in a hurry as if you are holding up proceedings while they attend to the Queen of Sheba or somebody equally more important.

"Is sir dining alone?" they ask smarmily.

"No, no I'm just waiting for two elephants and kangaroo," you wish to reply, but meekly nod and they make a great fuss of waving through numerous tables to eventually place you in a small corner table with barely enough room on it for the cutlery, let alone a three-course meal. Still, it did offer a great view of the other tables and sure enough there is always a selection of interesting diners to watch while you munch your way through the selection of fare on offer.

If it's an airport hotel or similar you are staying in, they tend to be full of single business diners or groups of three or four mismatched travellers, with the odd holiday couple or family thrown in. Odd is the right word. Aren't we a weird and wonderful species? City centre hotels generally throw up a far more varied selection of guests, some considerably more interesting than others, and then, of course, there's me in the midst of all these.

Why is it that the waiters insist on giving you a selection of hard, poppy-seeded and squashed rolls to amuse yourself with until they think you are actually ready to eat? I never have success with these things and should never touch them, but there they sit, in the middle of the table, waiting to taunt me. I choose one and try to slice it open with what looks like a knife but is in fact a blunt ice-pick. I saw away at this object, spreading poppy seeds everywhere and finally, in desperation, I grip the thing and tear it apart.

After that comes the butter. No little knobs of freshly patted, yellow, pasta-shaped tubes, but instead a plate full of small, rectangular, gold-paper-wrapped lumps of a frozen white substance. These I try to prise open, and invariably the slippery thing shoots out of my hands and across the table onto the floor. I know I should leave it there and try another packet, but no, I slide downwards in my seat and try to recover it with my foot, waving a long leg around underneath the tablecloth, like a fishing rod. After a few unsuccessful attempts the butter is now farther away, and I slide a tad further down in the seat, to the extent that I am now down around eye level with the table top and clinging on to the same table while trying to hoist the sides of the cloth up to get a better view. Again the swinging foot makes contact, and sends the butter way out the other side.

At this moment, I am suddenly aware of a waiter by my side... *"Everything alright, sir?"*

Startled by this intrusion into my world I jump up and smack the table with my knee, causing a loud clatter as the spare cutlery disappears over the side, and I very nearly take the tablecloth and everything on it with me! But I manage to straighten things out a bit, and nod quietly to this apparition by my side, *"Yes, yes thank you, everything's fine."*

"Would sir like to order now?"

Having been concentrating on the 'fishing for butter' programme I have lost all train of thought on the food side, and have to scurry through the menu and finally choose my courses for the night. He wafts off to the kitchen and I notice as he strides away a small gold rectangle stuck to the sole of his left foot... I decide I will just try another packet of butter for the mutilated roll lying on my side-plate. Eventually I extricate the white blob, place it in the centre of the roll and, pressing firmly with my knife, I manage to squeeze it into a slightly larger rectangle. This is as far as it goes so I munch my way through mostly dry bread with an overly large section of hard butter.

The seafood soup is creamy and very tasty and so is the main course. Possibly meringues and strawberries are not the best choice for dessert, but you have to live dangerously when dining alone. As soon as you offer your spoon to the meringues you just know that there will be an explosion like a party popper and you and the next table go on to share a small cloud of flaky particles together, which makes them all look as if they have just had an attack of dandruff. Still, all is well, and after the excitement of the meal, you think it best to just have a few beers in the bar and retire to bed with a good book.

This is often the time when you encounter one of the most dangerous machines in the hotel – the shoe-cleaning machine. These are generally situated in lobbies at the end of corridors, awaiting unsuspecting travellers emerging from the lifts late at night. I cannot go past them, especially after a couple of beers. You look at your shoes, all scuffed and messy from a day's travelling, possibly even coated in a thin layer of butter, and you just know you need to give them a clean. Firstly, you shove your feet, one at a time, into the polish coating bit and, while slightly aggressive, it manages to do the job and your shoes emerge with a dull coating of shoe polish on them ready for the next stage. And this, for me, is when things start to get exciting. I lean back and place my polish-coated shoe into the buffer wheels and the thing starts up with a vengeance. Slowly but surely, I try to keep my balance while this machine starts to eat my leg. In a flash it has drawn my shoe and trousers into its jaws and is devouring them at enormous speed. I try to stand on one leg, while dragging my half-eaten foot out of this contraption, but it's too strong and starts to sway about, as I do too. There is nothing to hold on to and we start to career around the corridor, dancing madly together while the zombie whines loudly and gulps down my shoe, with me hopping wildly behind it. Suddenly I trip and in a second am lying face down on the floor, one foot in the machine, the other scrabbling around trying to get a grip on the carpet, and the blessed thing bouncing around the lobby, ricocheting off the walls and into the upright metal ashtray in the corner. The noise is deafening and doors start to open and heads appear, squinting down the passage as they espy this character appearing to have his way with a dwarf robot in the middle of the floor.

At this point the lift doors open and out step a young couple, arm in arm, heading for their room and a romantic moment, to be confronted with an elderly, grey-haired man – glasses askew, clothes half off, writhing about on the floor, seemingly fighting off an attack by some electric crocodile – yelling and gesticulating wildly at them to... *"Pull out the plug! Pull out the plug!"*

She seems more in control of the situation than he is and runs across the landing and yanks the plug out of the socket. I then manage to extricate my mangled leg and shoe from the beast and eventually escape its clutches. I crawl about on all fours, finally getting to my feet, straightening my glasses and tucking my shirt back into my trousers. For such a carry on! I stop and thank her profusely, but politely refuse her offer of medical help and say I'll be fine. But I make a mental note to have a quiet word with reception in the morning about the pterodactyl they have lurking in their hotel corridors!

The life of the lone traveller is fraught with danger, and that's before you step outside and into the big wide world. Is it any wonder that travel insurance seems to get more expensive the older you get... or is it just me?

Wii and Me

Last Christmas, in a moment of wild passion and instability, we purchased a Wii system complete with the Wii Sports Pack or whatever it's called. This was after having its virtues extolled to us by all and sundry, and also a way of experiencing a downhill ski in the comfort and relative safety of a living room.

Now I don't know if you have one of these modern computer-generated games in your possession, but my word, these things can be dangerous at times. I cannot but think that there will be an EU directive issued shortly on the correct and safe usage of these items. It's not that they are dangerous in themselves, it's more that the user may or may not be fully aware of the implications of strapping a remote control to their wrist and letting fly all around the room.

Between Christmas and New Year we duly got the box out and emptied its contents all over the floor. After a reasonably short time I had mastered the diagrams and had plugged in the scart sockets and trailed cables and bits to a small control unit which sat on the floor beside the television, and attached a smart little sensor thingy to the top of the set. We then switched on the TV – and not unlike the heady days of yesteryear when we got our first automatic washing machine and sat transfixed in front of it, watching through a round porthole our clothes swirl round and round in a mass of foam and bubbles – we similarly sat in front of the set and waited. After a few re-reads of the instructions we'd mastered it, and up came a 'set-up' screen which allowed us to design a person who could be me and closely resembled a police 'identikit' picture.

We were now ready for the sports choices and initially we had the option of tennis, baseball, bowling, golf and, interestingly, boxing. You have to try them all, of course, and I mastered the tennis, ten-pin bowling and the golf and made a passable attempt at the baseball, even though I had no idea what the rules really were. But then I decided to have a go at the boxing! Well, the clever little computer boffins have devised a method whereby you are armed with two of these controller things, one of which is called a 'nunchuk'. Who came up with that name? I gather this is the title given to some weird martial art weapon, consisting of two wooden sticks and a piece of chain, that Bruce Lee used to prance about the screen waving at folks.

But whether the Wii designers pinched that name or not, I like to think it was maybe a group of marketing gurus sitting around going, *"Well, what do we call this thing, then?"*

And some guy says, *"A controller 2?"*

And the other smart kids look at one another and roll their eyes and go, *"Oh, for God's sake, Jim, you big nunchuk, we've got to do better than that!"*

"Heh... Dave, that's it...! Nunchuk, that's what we'll call it!"

Anyway, armed with my controller and nunchuk, it took a bit of time to get the hang of this co-ordinated two-handed approach and I was subsequently floored within seconds of taking up my southpaw stance, even though I'm not left-handed. Determined to get the better of the machine, I started moving swiftly about the floor, getting in the odd punch now and again. Well, Mohammed Ali didn't have a look in as I warmed up to this 'game'. I darted and dived about the floor and nipped in under his guard and BANG! I'd floored him and was the champion!

What a carry on though. I was sweating and pretty exhausted and I have to say it's some workout, if you want to make it that.

As I stood there perspiring and puffing with my controller and nunchuk in my trembling hands, I was aware of the cat, Elwood, sitting up on the chair as far back as he could go, pressed right into the cushions, with a huge wide-eyed, scared-as-hell look in his eyes. He'd just witnessed a grown man leaping and jumping around the sitting room, in front of the TV, all alone, with two small pieces of plastic in his hands, grunting and shouting and punching the air while ducking and diving from side to side, avoiding these invisible objects that seemed to shoot out from the big coloured box in the corner. Is it any wonder he was a trifle traumatised?

While we're on the subject of sport and fitness and the like, I have to tell you that I'm progressing well in the tennis, having reached the dizzy heights of skill level 1,000 or 'Pro' as they like to designate you. This comes at some sacrifice, I have to say, though. I'm not a fanatic as such and just have a go now and again when the mood takes me, and while I'm not obsessed with it, it does get a grip of you and you strive to outplay the little identikit morons on the screen. You also begin to question the line judges' decisions and are amazed that your 'opponents' can manage to return some of your classic Federer shots. It's you against them; it's not a computer disc anymore. Your pride is at stake here, for goodness sake. The only thing is that as you get into it a bit more you begin to wildly gesticulate and swipe violently at the ball, while charging around the room whooping and hollering.

It must have been at this point... I swished a beautiful forehand smash across the court into the far corner, but the little moustached model managed to get a return in and back it came... I just wasn't really ready for that, having thought I'd won the game with my powerful volley... and being ever so slightly off balance, I lurched madly at the 'ball', and tripped...

The insurance company were quite nice about it all. I have to say the description of the events leading up to the fall made interesting reading and I'm sure the guys at Legal and General had a laugh. I'm only glad the windows are made from very strong double-glazing as I didn't actually expect the controllers to bounce back so far. They really are made from amazingly hard plastic and quite sore when they ricochet off your face. To be honest, the pet insurance didn't seem to cover 'being stood on', though Elwood's fine now... but as soon as I reach for the box with the Wii controllers in it he's out the door faster than a bullet. Floats like a butterfly, stings like a bee...

As a sort of addendum to this story, we recently purchased the Wii Fit Plus pack, which includes the downhill slalom skiing, snowboarding, ski jumping, and a few other 'balance' exercises, as it likes to calls them. These all involve using the 'balance board' and one in particular requires you to attempt to head off a series of footballs which are fired at you, together with a collection of football boots. Obviously, you are supposed to avoid the boots and head the balls. To do this you stand on the board and weave about, alternatively squatting, leaning, swerving, and all the time head-butting the ever-faster approaching avalanche of balls and boots.

It was at this time a new Streamline delivery driver passed by our front window trying to find our one and only entrance door. He was greeted by the sight of me standing in the middle of the room – no other person to hand, and no sound emanating from the TV which had it's back to the window – twisting and turning, ducking and diving, in ever-increasing circles, with a weird grimace on my face as, unknown to him, every now and then a football boot smacked me between the eyes and I let fly with an oath.

Eventually he caught my attention, with a slightly terrified look on his face, and I pointed around the house to where the door was. I got there and opened it to find him standing a good six feet away from the door, holding out a Next package at arm's length. I signed for it and he walked very quickly away, glancing back every now and then. Weird guy, I thought. It was only after I came back into the sitting room that I realised what he would have seen and began to understand his actions!

To make it even more understandable, when I clicked on finish for the 'game' the nice lady personal trainer announced to me on the screen that I was 'unbalanced'. That figures.

Roll me Over

Having had a few stories written about me or involving my good self, I thought it was time I, Elwood the cat, took over the keyboard again and outlined a small story as seen from my angle.

Today I am recovering. This happens to me a lot nowadays, as I have to take time out after some of my exploits. This is a process of recharging the batteries after some over exuberant aerobics. Yesterday I was moving with the speed of light... and today, I resemble a sloth on half speed.

I enjoy little moments of extreme exploration whereby I can vault up onto the oil tank from where I can deftly span the gap between this and the house, and so climb upwards towards the ridge. This is an exciting moment and I then take up a spate of free-running along the ridgeline, chasing unsuspecting starlings. These guys are really stupid.

Recently I had a sublime moment of living life as nature intended, stalking an elusive starling that had chosen to sit atop the chimney. I enjoy these early morning, dawn arising stealth patrols. They keep me sharp and in tune with the environment.

I had ascended the roof by means of the oil tank and the cute little starling was sitting there with his back to me, unaware of my approach. I shuffled along the ridge flat on my belly, SAS style, and crept up behind him. The silly article was tweeting away big time, so helping to drown out any noises I may have made as I drew closer and closer. I did have one slightly dangerous moment when I was momentarily distracted by a low-flying fat pigeon, who turned and dive-bombed me in an attempt to dislodge me from my flattened ridge position. He very nearly succeeded too, as I made a quick swipe at him as he screamed past, though I missed and toppled over the ridge... but I grabbed out with both paws and dug in with my claws, and managed to hold on. He's on my list of 'take-outs' now... I'll remember him too... fat, grey with a hint of purple, and one red eye. His days are numbered!

I have to confess, I am not the most successful predator, having so far in my long life managed to catch just one very small rabbit, which I didn't have the heart to kill and just slipped into the utility room for a bit of fun one day. Dear God, the mass hysteria that caused! Speak about being useless. Humans just don't seem to be able to get it together when small rodents invade their space. For crying out loud! They're a hundred times their size, but they jump about and stamp the ground and scream and shout, none of which does any good. Why they don't just bend down and pick the little devils up with their teeth, give them a couple of vicious shakes and it would all be over. But no, they get cardboard boxes and brooms and run around trying to sweep them up or bash them over the head. It never works and they generally smash something or other and break windows. Still, it's great to watch, and just proves that we cats are the 'supreme being'.

Anyhow, back to the ridge. Smartypants starling is still there, singing his heart out on the chimney top. I am now within inches of him and coil myself into the athletic form I am and lean back... and leap! Maybe my timing was a tad off, or possibly he had got wind of my approach, but in the half light of the morning I didn't quite notice the wire stay which supports the metal chimney... and I catapulted into that which sent a loud 'twang' through the air. The next sequence of events was quite spectacular, if a trifle worrying. The starling jumped upwards and promptly hit his head on the chimney can and toppled backwards down the chimney! I, in turn, had spanged off the wire support, smacked my head against the same chimney can and fell backwards down the roof. I scrabbled frantically at the tiles and just managed to grab hold of the last one, but the momentum carried me onwards and I lost my grip. I was now within inches of the roof edge and with an almighty twist and turn I sprang through the air and landed heavily on the oil tank roof. Another 'hunting' moment gone awry... once more!

I took a moment to assess things and my position, and was actually quite chuffed that I still had that inbuilt sense of balance and dexterity to fly through the air and land feet first when faced with imminent death. I took a moment to lick my backside, as you do in situations like this, and then lay back with a large grin on my face, rolled over, and promptly fell backwards off the tank and landed in among the rose bushes! Not a pretty sight. I shot upwards from there with a few thorns stuck in places thorns shouldn't go, and tried to walk nonchalantly off the flower bed as if nothing had happened. The starlings on the fence wire broke into a huge round of laughter and they mockingly tweeted loudly at me as I ambled off.

Hah... but I had the last laugh, their brother had been forced down the chimney by Elwood the Destroyer... I was still ahead on points. However, I began to realise this may cause large amounts of distress to the humans, as the chimney was attached directly to the wood stove, and there was no means of escape for the said starling. I took a stroll across to the patio door and from this excellent vantage point I could see directly into the sitting room. There in front of me was the glass-fronted wood stove, with a small frantic looking bird darting about inside the fire. It being the summer there were no flames, just an empty grate... and a blackened dancing starling.

Things could only get better... it was just an hour or so before the humans would be getting up, so I settled down to a short nap before the excitement and fun would commence. I didn't have to wait long as, sure enough, I awoke to see the man of the house coming into the room in his usual early morning gait, ambling around in his boxers looking out on the sea and down towards the beach. Oh, goodie, goodie... wait till he checks the fire... yip, here he goes, his attention drawn to the noise of the starling doing back flips behind the glass door.

"*Good God... what's that?*" he mutters to himself. "*Oh, my God, it's a bird. How the hell did it get in there?*"

He stands and looks at it, while the starling stops his aerobics and similarly stands, head cocked to one side, and looks back at him. A stand-off ensues. He then sees me looking in at the patio doors and comes across and opens them to let me in. I feign love and affection by weaving between his legs and then edge up to the fire for a closer look. Hee, hee! What a cracker. The bird gives me the eye and I give him my fiercest twitching-mouth bristling-whiskers look, and pretend to paw at the door.

"*Heh!*" the Mr says, "*come away from the fire. How are we going to get him out of there?*" he asks nobody but himself, as he doesn't realise I can understand him.

You've got your work cut out there pal, I think to myself, but hell, it's going to be a lot of fun watching this.

He ambles off and in a minute the Mrs of the house returns with him. They both look down at the starling who is now into his *Dirty Dancing* routine, jiving back and fore inside the grate, kicking up the ash and dust and generally making a right meal of it.

A few minutes pass while they both look at the bird and the fire, and a lot of muttering goes on until, finally, he heads off out of the room, only to return a few minutes later with a large dustsheet. Oh, wow... this looks good! He proceeds to describe in minute detail to her the intricacies of the capture manoeuvre. It sounds too good to be true. He thinks if he deftly opens the door a mere fraction and positions himself close by with the sheet, when the starling makes his escape he will capture the bird in the sheet and then release it outside. Simples! Ho ho...!

She takes up position on the door handle; he in squatting, poised, dustsheet-at-the-ready stance. The fun is about to start. I retreat a few steps behind as I just know this is never going to work, but I might just be able to nip in and capture the starling with a quick pounce if he tries to make a get away. Slowly, ever so slowly, she cranks open the fire door and he is now moving slightly closer... a bit further... but still no bird appears... a bit wider the door opens and still no sign of the little devil. Finally, she opens it completely and looks inside. He's nowhere to be seen... this is clever... what's he done? I take a step nearer too and both of us are now peering into the fire grate. He must have climbed in behind the throat plate or something like that... and the Mrs and me look at one another, and just as we look back into the fire... he leaps out from behind the plate and makes a dash for freedom.

Holy shit, all hell breaks loose! She falls backwards with fright at the bird flying past her nose, he steps on the dustsheet and tries to throw it over the speeding feathered object, trips himself up and lands in a heap on the loose mat, which shoots outwards and results in him upending himself onto the floor and throwing the dustsheet over his wife. She scrabbles about underneath it while he rolls over on the mat and lunges desperately at the zooming starling. I, to show willingness, give a couple of swipes at it as it flies past, which does make it alter it's flight path considerably and it goes on to head-butt the patio door quite forcibly. He leaps up to try and catch the stunned bird, and I join in the merry frolics but, possibly, I am not helping matters as he inadvertently trips over me and disappears over the back of the settee, in what I have to say is a beautiful manoeuvre, somewhat reminiscent of a swan landing on a loch.

There is a tremendous crash from behind the sofa, and I guess there's no water there to absorb his landing. Mrs, meanwhile, has finally extricated herself from the dustsheet and is chasing the bird around the sitting room. He appears to be trying to get up again, as a few grunting sounds come from behind the sofa, and slowly his dishevelled head appears above the backrest. I have taken this moment to slip quietly away and take up a position near the opposite window, sitting with my mouth as wide open as I can in the faint hope the starling will fly directly into it. This doesn't happen as, while the bird is heading in my direction, so are the humans, armed with the dustsheet amid cries of despair as they dart round and round the room chasing the blasted thing.

I have to say, I haven't had so much fun since the day they tried to give me a tablet, and I watch in amazement as the chase ensues. The final and ultimate tactic is a clever one in a way, but not necessarily the best for all concerned. He decides to open the patio door as wide as he can, while she tries to steer the wild-eyed, high-speed, super jet Mr Starling towards the opening. Three aborted attempts later, they are closing in on the beast and a concentrated effort on their part with the dustsheet is the plan. They shoot past me, holding the sheet high between them above their heads, and driving the bird towards the open door. The bird finally dives down and out into the open air... so, too, does he... with the sheet over his head... he shoots out and lands on the cold concrete in his bare feet... concrete which is littered with small, sharp, white stones. Not as was initially planned, I think!

The story of the 7.30am bus seeing a ghostly vision outside a Levenwick house as it cruised past was told for many a day. Not only was this apparition flaying about but it was seen to be jumping wildly up and down too, and with a blood-curdling wail emanating from within. A fearsome sight!

Later, talk at breakfast was all about 'the flaming bird', or words to that effect, and how it could have fallen down the chimney. I lay there at the side of the Rayburn saying nothing... but I knew... because a little bird had told me!